Mr. Florentine's Violin

Written by John Parsons
Illustrated by Kerry Gemmill

Contents	Page
Chapter 1. *A beautiful courtyard*	4
Chapter 2. *Mr. Florentine's music*	11
Chapter 3. *Some good news*	17
Chapter 4. *A surprise!*	23
Chapter 5. *A thank-you present*	29
Verse	32

Mr. Florentine's Violin

With these characters ...

Mr. Florentine

Marco

Bella

Gino

"Eeeeek! A shriek

Setting the scene ...

In the Italian city of Venice, three restaurants are full of happy people. They are enjoying the sounds of the city and the water — until suddenly, a terrible sound fills the air.

What is going on in the apartment above the restaurants? Is Mr. Florentine in trouble? His friends rush to find out!

filled the air!"

Chapter 1.

"Via Luna" is the name of a narrow street in Venice, Italy. Its name means "Moon Street" in Italian. On Via Luna there was a tiny courtyard where three restaurants cooked the best food in Venice.

People ate at tables in the courtyard. They could see gondolas gliding slowly up and down the canal. They listened to the clocks chiming every hour. And on this night, the moon glistened in the water. People said everything was "bella", which means "beautiful" in Italian.

One Saturday night, there were no empty restaurant tables. Waiters carried plates in and out of the kitchens. Delicious smells filled the air. The sound of the water from the canal filled the courtyard. People were relaxed and happy.

"Eeeeek!" A shriek filled the air! The loud sound echoed around the courtyard. The three restaurant owners rushed outside to find out where the shriek was coming from. They wondered what could be wrong.

Marco, the owner of the first restaurant, wondered if someone had found a slimy slug in their salad.

Bella, the owner of the second restaurant, wondered if a cook had cut a finger!

Gino, the owner of the third restaurant, wondered if someone had broken a tooth.

"Waaaah!" Another horrible shriek filled the air! Who was shrieking? Where was that terrible sound coming from?

Marco looked up. The sound was coming from a window above his restaurant!

"Quick, Bella! Polizi! Call the police!" yelled Marco.

"And call an ambulance, too!" added Gino.

Marco and Gino ran up the stairs toward an apartment. It sounded like something terrible was happening inside!

Chapter 2.

"Run faster, before we're too late!" yelled Gino. He puffed as he ran behind Marco. "Si spicci!" he called, which means "hurry up" in Italian.

At the top of the stairs, Gino and Marco reached a green door. With one big shove, they pushed the door open — just like in the movies!

Inside the apartment, there was an old man, with gray hair and a beard. He sat by the window in a huge, green armchair.

Under his chin he held an old violin. In his right hand, he held an old violin bow.

"Marco? Gino? What's the matter?" he said, sounding shocked.

"Mr. Florentine, don't worry!" puffed Marco. "The police are coming!"

"Mr. Florentine, don't worry!" panted Gino. "An ambulance will be here soon, too!"

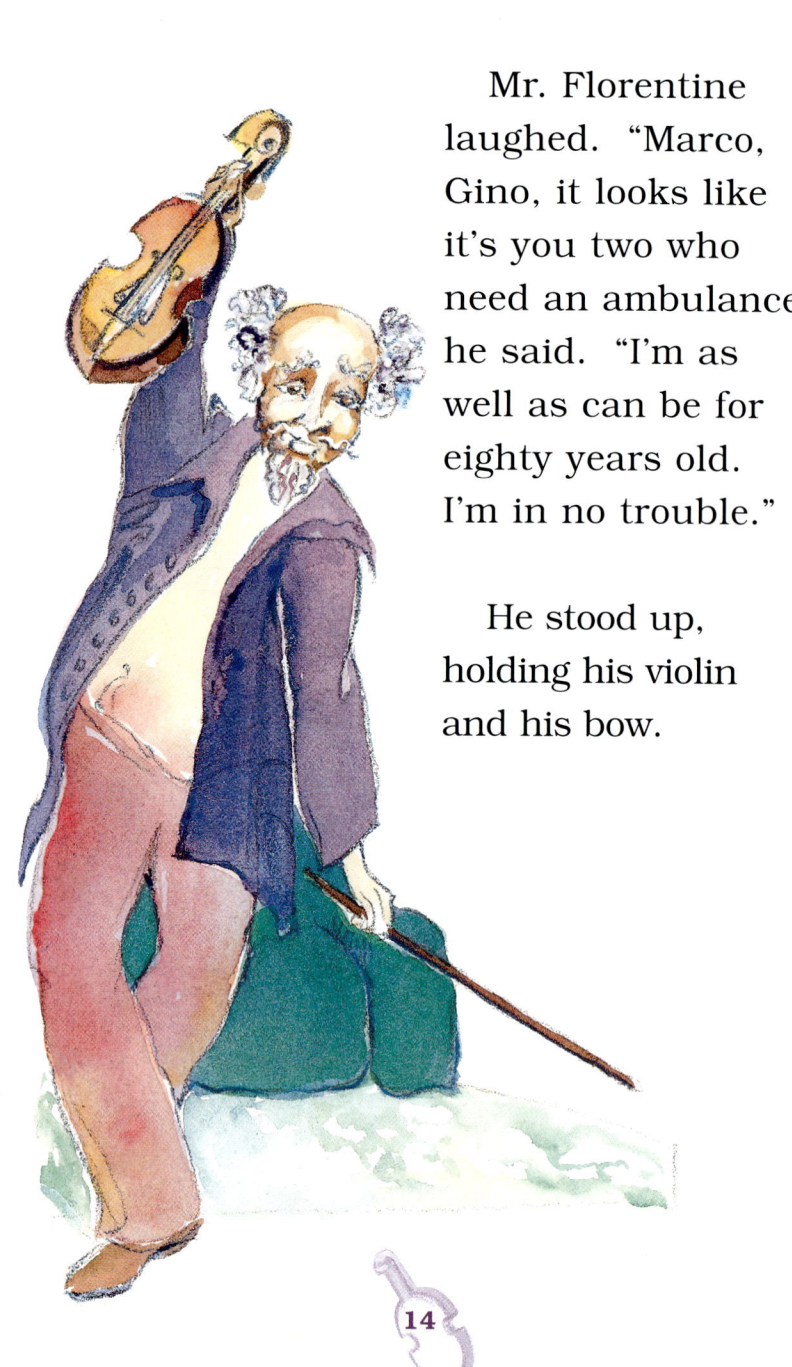

Mr. Florentine laughed. "Marco, Gino, it looks like it's you two who need an ambulance," he said. "I'm as well as can be for eighty years old. I'm in no trouble."

He stood up, holding his violin and his bow.

"I'm learning to play the violin," he smiled. "I have plenty of spare time to learn now."

Gino and Marco looked shocked. Mr. Florentine moved the bow across the violin strings. The same shrieking sound swirled through the room, out the window, around the courtyard below, and out over the canal.

Marco and Gino clapped their hands over their ears.

"I do need to practice more," admitted Mr. Florentine, smiling.

Just then, Bella, a policeman, and two ambulance attendants burst into the room. Marco and Gino looked embarrassed. Mr. Florentine smiled, but he didn't stop his violin practice. Everyone left the room *very* quickly!

Chapter 3.

Every evening for the next two weeks, the restaurants' customers had to listen to Mr. Florentine's violin. On and on and on it shrieked, squealed, and squeaked. People couldn't hear each other speak. The waiters could not concentrate and mixed up everyone's orders.

Bella, Gino, and Marco frowned. This was bad for everyone's business!

"Mr. Florentine is too old to learn anything new," thought Marco. Now he had to put earplugs on the tables, next to the forks.

"He'll never learn to play that violin," thought Bella. She had to give people pens and paper to write down what they wanted to say.

"All that practice is not working," thought Gino, tripping over a chair leg.

After three weeks of awful violin practice, the restaurant owners had a meeting. Customers were staying away from their restaurants. Mr. Florentine had to be stopped!

"Marco! Bella! Gino! How nice of you to visit me," said Mr. Florentine, politely.

"Mr. Florentine, we're sorry, but we're here to speak to you about your violin practice," said Bella softly.

Mr. Florentine looked sad. "Yes, I'm sorry, too," he said. "I have some bad news."

The restaurant owners looked worried. What did Mr. Florentine mean? Was he going to start playing the trumpet? Or the drums?

"I'm afraid you will not hear my music for the next three months," he said. "I am going to a music school in Rome to learn more about the violin."

Marco, Bella, and Gino tried to look sad, too. Three months without shrieks, squeals, and squeaks! Yes!

"You all look disappointed," said Mr. Florentine. "Don't worry, I will be back," he said happily. After hearing this news, the restaurant owners *did* look disappointed.

Chapter 4.

After one month, the restaurant tables had happy customers eating at them again. Waiters no longer mixed up orders. The sounds of the city and the water lapping on stones filled the courtyard once again.

After two months, Marco, Gino, and Bella became worried. What would they do when Mr. Florentine returned?

"Let's ask all our customers to sign a petition to stop him from playing his violin," suggested Bella.

Marco and Gino agreed. It was a sensible plan. For the next month, they collected signatures from every customer. Soon, they had hundreds of signatures on their petition. No one wanted shrieks, squeals, or squeaks to spoil their dinner again.

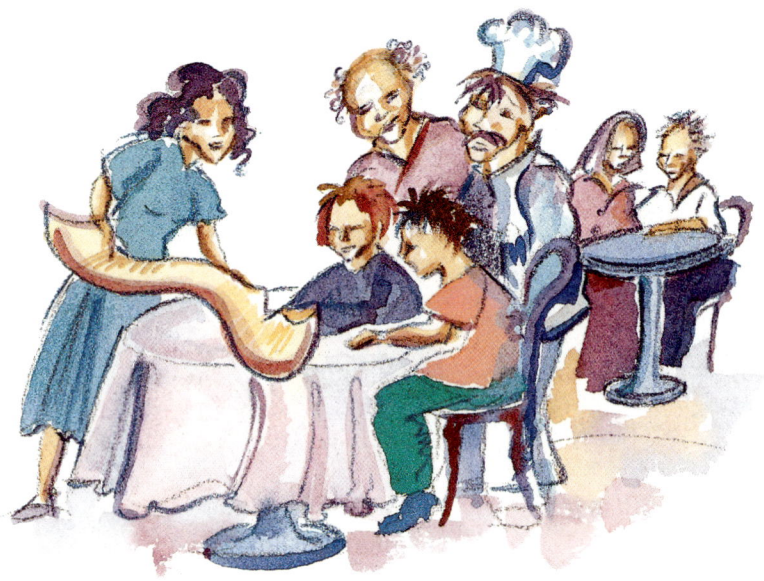

When Mr. Florentine returned from music school, he waved at everyone as he walked upstairs to his apartment. The restaurant owners were worried when Mr. Florentine's window opened.

As Mr. Florentine tuned his violin, a tiny shriek came from the window. A short squeak echoed around the courtyard. A low squeal was heard across the canal.

Marco, Gino, and Bella took their petition and walked toward Mr. Florentine's apartment. They didn't want to hurt his feelings, but they didn't want Mr. Florentine's violin playing to keep people away from their restaurants, either.

Then, slowly and softly, a beautiful tune floated out of Mr. Florentine's window. Soaring, sweet music swept around the courtyard like a fresh spring breeze. The restaurant owners stopped walking and listened. They couldn't believe what they were hearing.

Mr. Florentine's violin sang like a bird in springtime. His music floated out over the canal and up toward the full moon. The people in the restaurants stopped eating just to enjoy the music.

Marco, Gino, and Bella walked back to an empty table and sat there listening. They sat there all evening, too astounded to say a word. Everyone else sat there all evening, too, until all the candles had burned down, and Mr. Florentine finished playing.

The restaurant owners threw their petition in the trash. Somehow, the sound of the city, the water, and Mr. Florentine's beautiful violin music made their courtyard seem perfect.

Chapter 5.

Within weeks, everyone in Venice wanted to hear Mr. Florentine's music. Business was booming at the restaurants.

One summer evening, Marco, Gino, and Bella wanted to give Mr. Florentine a thank-you present. They knocked gently on his door.

When Mr. Florentine saw the beautiful new violin, he had tears in his eyes. He was speechless. All he could say was, "Magnifico." And all he did was sit by his window and play even more beautifully than before.

  Even today, in Venice, you may hear
Mr. Florentine's violin. Drift along
a canal, by the light of the full moon.
Follow the sound of a far-away violin.
If you are lucky, it will lead you to
a narrow street like Via Luna.
There, you may find someone to show
you why you're never too old to learn
something new!

"A Lovely Tune-a"

A man who once lived on Via Luna
Played his violin under the moon.
He went off to Rome,
And when he came home,
He'd learned how to play
A lovely tune!